BEDTIME!

by Ruth Freeman Swain

illustrated by Cat Bowman Smith

Holiday House / New York

For my three boys
R. F. S.

In memory of Thomas
C. B. S.

Text copyright © 1999 by Ruth Freeman Swain
Illustrations copyright © 1999 by Cat Bowman Smith
All Rights Reserved
Printed in the United States of America
First Edition

Library of Congress Cataloging-in-Publication Data
Swain, Ruth Freeman.
Bedtime!/by Ruth Freeman Swain; illustrated by Cat Bowman Smith.
p. cm.
Summary: Relates a variety of facts about beds, sleepwear, and sleeping
from different cultures and periods of history, from ancient Egypt and China
to the contemporary world of astronautics.
ISBN 0-8234-1444-2
1. Sleeping customs—Juvenile literature. 2. Bedtime—Juvenile literature.
[1. Beds. 2. Bedtime. 3. Sleeping customs.]
I. Smith, Cat Bowman, ill. II. Title.
GT3000.3.S83 1999
392.3'6—dc21   98-56076
CIP

When we go to bed, we are doing something that people have done for thousands of years. Maybe we lie on mattresses, while earlier people lay on mats. We plump up pillows, while they fluffed up straw. We burrow under blankets, while they burrowed under furs. But we all go to bed. We all need to rest.

Ancient Egyptians kept cool by sleeping on wooden bed frames strung with cords to let air pass through. Hard headrests were cooler than pillows but not as soft!

Because living on the banks of the Nile meant mosquitoes, everyone slept with mosquito netting, even King Tutankhamen on his golden bed. Fishermen who couldn't afford mosquito netting crept under their fishing nets at night.

In ancient China, houses had raised platforms called kíangs, where families ate and slept together. The kíang was heated from underneath by hot air from a small heater.

For pillows, the Chinese used hard headrests to protect the fancy hairstyles of the adults. Children's pillows were covered with fabric, and were sometimes in the shapes of animals who would keep watch at night with wide open eyes.

During the Middle Ages in Europe a "bed" was the mattress, cushions, and hanging curtains that went on and around a simple wooden box called a bedstead. When lords and ladies traveled from one castle to another, they took their beds with them but left their bedsteads behind.

At bedtime everyone crawled into bed together. No one slept alone
unless he or she was very important or very sick. Nightgowns were clothes
worn at night but taken off before getting into bed.

Hammocks are hanging beds. They were used in Central and South America long before Columbus arrived in the New World. Woven from plant fibers, they kept sleepers cool, and above whatever was creeping or crawling on the ground.

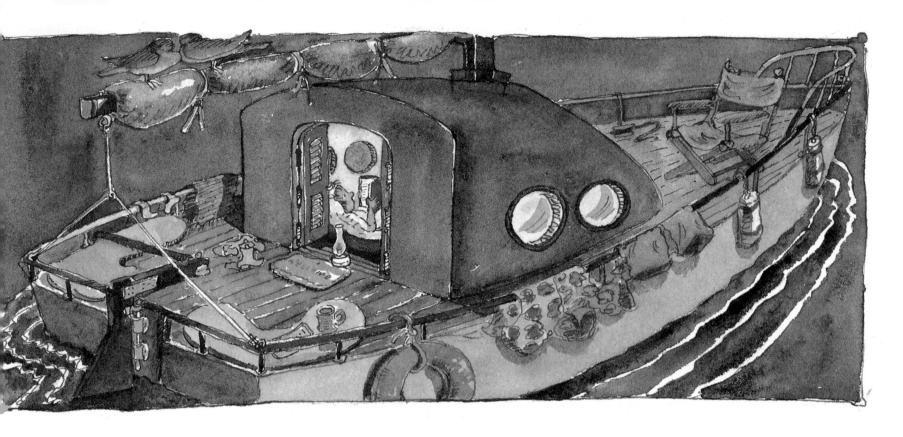

Today, hammocks are used in many countries. Some people sleep in hammocks every night; others lie in them on lazy afternoons.

In Europe during the sixteenth and seventeenth centuries some beds were very fancy and some were very big. The biggest bed is the Great Bed of Ware. It is twelve feet wide and twelve feet long. It was made for an inn in England. Many people came to the inn just to see the bed that could hold ten or twelve people at once.

King Louis XIV of France owned 413 beds. At his palace in Versailles his bed stood behind a golden fence with a little gate. The bed canopy was topped with white ostrich plumes. Magnificent beds like this one often reached higher than a basketball net.

In the nineteenth century across Europe and America new ideas and inventions began to change the way beds looked. When extra space was needed, people could buy beds that folded into cupboards, bookcases, or even pianos. A Murphy bed is a bed that completely disappears into a closet.

Another new idea was an old idea in India. Travelers returning home to Europe from India brought something with them we still use today: pajamas.

Millions of people came to the United States by ship in the nineteenth and early twentieth centuries. Many of them traveled in steerage, the space below deck. The air was hot and stuffy since there were no portholes to let in light and air. Beds were narrow bunk beds, stacked three or four high, set in rows. Everything you brought for your new life in America was stored on your bunk.

Before airplanes, the fastest way to cross the United States was by train. The trip from coast to coast lasted about four days and three nights.

In Pullman sleeping cars, seats were arranged back to back on either side of the aisle by day. At night the porter changed the seats into a lower berth, or bed, and pulled down the upper berth from the ceiling. Heavy "Pullman green" curtains were hung, making each bed snug and cozy.

Next time you're on a highway, take a look at the trucks that haul loads long distances. A lot of them have a sleeper compartment behind the driver's seat. The driver can park and go to bed in the truck or, if the driver has a partner, one can sleep while the other drives.

Two hundred miles above the Earth, traveling at 17,000 miles an hour, astronauts can get a good night's sleep.

How do people stay cool on a really hot summer night? At the edge of the Sahara desert where temperatures can reach 140 degrees Fahrenheit (60 degrees Centigrade), the Berbers live underground where it is cool and moist.

Their pit homes are twenty feet under the ground and have rooms for people and animals. Beds are laid in shelves carved into the walls. If another bed is needed, a shelf is easily dug into the soft earth.

Keeping warm in bed has been a problem for a long time. Sleeping bags, first used by the Inuit in the Arctic, are taken by mountain climbers on a long climb. They sleep on special hanging platforms and wear harnesses attached to the rock wall so they can be safe thousands of feet above the ground.

Through the years babies have slept in hollowed-out logs, in baskets, cradles, and cribs. They have slept in hospital incubators.

They have slept in trundle beds that pulled out from underneath their parents' bed. At least one baby has slept in a manger.

The Dakota/Lakota tribe, living on the Great Plains, put babies in cradle boards during the day if mothers were working or if the band was traveling. In tipis at night babies slept in buffalo robes, often with their grandmothers.

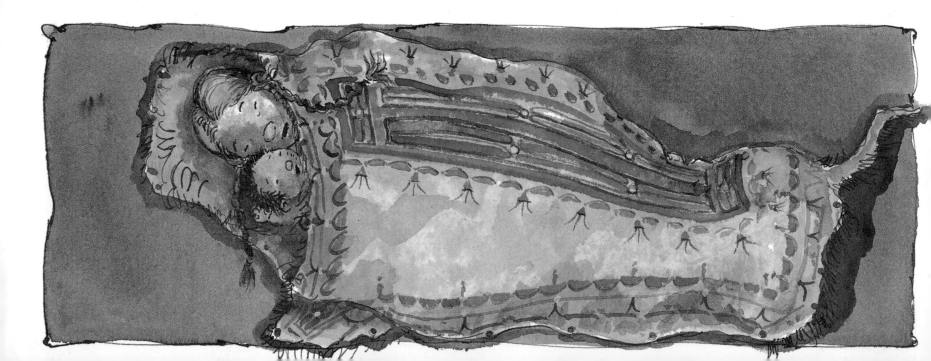

A bed is not just another piece of furniture. It's a place were we go to be alone, to read, or to feel better, as well as to sleep.

Whether you like your bed tucked in tight or all in a heap, filled with friends or only you, covered with blankets or quilts or nothing at all, there has never been another bed anywhere like yours.

Facts about Sleep

Sleeping is something we have in common with all mammals. It is something we do naturally, like breathing, eating, and going to the bathroom.

As we sleep, some parts of our bodies rest. Other parts, like our ears and brains, keep working. Hormones are released while we sleep and new cells are made.

Scientists continue to study what happens during sleep. One theory is that the brain uses the time to sift through the day's memories, storing some in long-term memory and discarding others. There are five stages of sleep; some are lighter periods of sleep, some are deeper. The Rapid Eye Movement state, or REM, which gets its name from the characteristic darting back and forth of the eyes while closed, is the dreaming stage. Everyone dreams several times a night even though most dreams are forgotten by morning.

Some people experience bad dreams (nightmares), sleepwalking, or night terrors (when someone appears wide awake and fearful or intent on doing something but has no memory of it later). Sleepwalking and night terrors occur during deep sleep and are not related to the dreaming stage.

We spend a third of our lives asleep, which is about 222,000 hours in an average life. If you put all your dreams together, they would add up to five or six years!

People sleep in different ways and at different times. On the other side of the world people are waking up as you are going to bed. Some people sleep in the daytime so they can work at night. Some people need more sleep than others, like 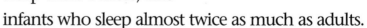 infants who sleep almost twice as much as adults.

Our brains are in charge of sleeping. Whether we fall asleep quickly or take a while, our brains watch over our bodies and make sure we get the amount of sleep we need. Sweet dreams!

Helpful Sources

DITTRICK, MARK. *The Bed Book: Over 100 Beds You Can Make, Buy, Order and Ogle.* New York: Harcourt Brace, 1980.

EDEN, MARY, AND RICHARD CARRINGTON. *The Philosophy of the Bed.* London: Spring Books, 1961.

HARRIS, EILEEN. *Going to Bed.* London: Victoria and Albert Museum, 1981.

HAYWARD, HELENA, editor. *World Furniture: An Illustrated History.* London and New York: Hamlyn Publishing Group, 1965.

KELLY, KEVIN, AND ERIN JAEB. *Sleep On It!* (A World of Difference series). Chicago: Children's Press Inc., 1995.

WRIGHT, LAWRENCE. *Warm and Snug: The History of the Bed.* London: Routledge and Kegan Paul, 1962.